TABLE OF CONTENTS

Foreword

Acknowledgement

Preface

CHAPTER 1   Career Guidance..8

CHAPTER 2   Recruitment Process..12

CHAPTER 3   Curriculum Vitae (CV)...21

CHAPTER 4   Application Letter 24

CHAPTER 5   The Interview Tips and Processes 30

CHAPTER 6   Percentage Of Respondents' Ratting..35

CHAPTER 7   Continuation Of Interview Processes..38

CHAPTER 8   Some Techniques and Preparation Tips (starting from Home)........44

CHAPTER 9   From The Main Entrance to the Interview Room 49

CHAPTER 10 Inside the Offices 53

CHAPTER 11 Psychological Tests For Candidates' Selection................................57

CHAPTER 12 The Interview Session (Interviewee versus Interviewer)................63

CHAPTER 13 Some Considerations 67

CHAPTER 14 Induction Process...71

CHAPTER 15 Internal Training Process...77

CHAPTER 16 Basic Principles Of Management...82

REFERENCES
....102

FOREWORD

I give honour to the mighty power of God and the Holy Spirit which strengthened me and became my candle bearer from the beginning up to the completion of this book; otherwise I could not have written anything.

At the time of writing I was employed by twelve deferent companies before and I was also interviewed quiet often. During this twelve time stint mostly at managerial level my duties involved interviewing job seekers. I was employed as lecturer twice.

I have pleasure in it that I am a clean holder of a prestigious Diploma in INTERNATIONAL TRADE which I obtained with a United Kingdom based WADE WORLD TRADE ORGANISATION (WWTO) in accreditation with DEBRECEN UNIVERSITY in HUNGARY with which I specialized in Import – Export Agency. I got registered in England as an Import-Export Agent and became a full member of WADE WORLD TRADE ORGANISATION (WWTO) with membership number **ZW12/0112/M9**.

I am also a clean holder of a Diploma in SALES and MARKETING MANAGEMENT with Diplomate number **RZ0476** with Certificates in SALES REPRESENTATIVE and MARKETING both obtained in ZIMBABWE.

On the social circles I serve in the community as the Chairman for Crime Consultative Committee (CCC) in Area 4 of the Zimbabwe Republic Police (ZRP) CHEGUTU District.

Had it not been passion and my vast practical-hands-on experience obtained over the years coupled with adequate training I could not have anything worth to write about. I have noted that most job seekers could fail interviews even before they enter the interview room mainly because of bad presentation, bad performance and inadequate preparation. That is what have pushed me to put pen on paper so that I equip would be job seekers through this Step-By-Step guide handbook that will take them through to successful interviews many times to come.

After having gone through this Handbook you will find every reason to keep it for future use as reference book.

I wish you well in your endeavour to pursue your chosen carrier and it is my prayer that whosoever gained access and read this Handbook will succeed in all his/her next interviews and become a wealthy bread winner.

MAY GOD BLESS AND LET YOU BECOME A JEWEL TO OTHERS

AUTHOR - Francis Mutimuri

ACKNOWLEDGEMENTS

AUTHOR: Sir Francis Mutimuri

EDITED BY: Dr Muchineripi T Ndewere

My first acknowledgement and thanks is dedicated to my wife Spiwe Mutimuri (nee Mangwiro) who gave me all the necessary moral support and advice. Many thanks also goes to my children, Edmund my eldest child who supported me technologically, Shalom, Charmain and the little one (at the time of writing) Chantal who never cried during the night time that I used to write this book. Special thanks also goes to Tsitsi Chakaza who provided me with a state-of-the-art Laptop for the typing of this book and she stood behind my project providing where possible all necessary support from start to finish. I thank Ortness Chakale a typist for her million dollar advice as she refused to type this book fearing for possible leakage preferring that I go it myself.

My foremost acknowledgement and honour is dedicated to Dr M T Ndewere who edited and perfected this book.

Above all I give my greatest thanks and honour to the Mighty God whose spirit was my anchor.

PREFACE

You are now about to be enriched with valuable educational resource and information that is fully packed with interview processes and techniques that will see you realize your dream and desired job. You will enjoy reading this book as it unpacks and outlines a smooth flow of interview events on a step-by-step basis.

An interview is the final process that lends you to your desired job; therefore, great care must be taken. It is how best you conduct yourself before, during and after the interview that will make it a success. Bearing in mind that it is the interviewer who will be expecting from the interviewee and not the other way round, therefore, special emphasis has been placed to structure this handbook to carefully and intelligently bolster you throughout the interview process in an interesting fashion. It was deliberately made short to enable one to read and finish it in a short pace of time.

This lecture handbook is written in English language that is easy to understand for everyone. It is purely designed to assist school leavers, College or University graduates, managers responsible for recruitment and anyone looking for employment or intending to move from one employment to another or climb higher at the same institution

A lot of emphasis has been placed on the practical aspect of the interview process. One will find this book fit enough to partner with throughout one's work life. It is by no doubt that one will need to consult with this book whenever he/she is called for an interview, so it is a necessary and perfect reference book.

It is a step-by-step, easy to follow and understand guide handbook with clear explanations and examples given to curb the eye of the mind to visualize the smooth flow of events. The book is also deliberately designed in such a way that will afford you a smile on your way back from the interview. This lecture handbook is enriched with valuable information while deliberately made short to enable you to read it to the end in a short pace of time.

It gives you hope, confidence and charisma Step-By-Step to successfully face all types of interviews in your future endeavours. It is designed in such an interesting fashion that will encourage one to go through all the topics. This handbook is specially written in such a unique way that will enlighten and gives you overview, insight and a complete reflection of what you will read and take care of in an interview right from start. **Now get you can get started and arm yourself**

BUY ONE or simply DOWNLOAD IT from the Internet

CHAPTER 1

CAREER GUIDANCE

DEFINITION

Career is defined as, 'a calling in life that is formed on the basis of an inner desire to pursue a certain course of education that will become inseparable to a one's occupation or profession.' Choosing a 'career' is a fall of heart and can be very dynamic as one can make some change of mind on the way as he or she grow. It must not be someone's choice also but, yours and, yours alone as it is what your heart desires. However, not overlooking the fact of receiving advises toward your chosen career, with some, advising against because of life's experiences; and it still remains with you to decide your course of action without being compelled to. Your dreams must always follow your career. Like life's interests, career also does change as one sees the good and bad things over a span of years that are or become associated with your chosen career.

WHAT LEADS TO CHANGES

For example; you may have had chosen and liked a certain career at an early age, but, over the span of years, that same job of your heart begin not to pay and those that are with it, virtually, are now languishing in poverty. It disheartens and dents one's prospects of a better future, therefore, as a result of that, the obvious thing becomes obvious; you dump the idea of working such a job, thus, calling for a change of mind and you chose another. There are many factors which can force one into making changes to his career and it will always be a strong reason to which one can base on. However, in most cases, one's career sees no obstacles and any change of mind must not be based on the remuneration factor alone; it should be broad based as things can change in your favour along the way and you will no longer be able to re-do what was undone because it could be too late and overtaken by events. Since "career" is founded from the heart – in normal circumstances people tend to soldier-on regardless of challenges met along the way.

THE BASIS OF CAREER

The basis of every career is its inseparability with one's heart and unless a person decides to make a change of heart it will also be very difficult to persuade that person to go against what he has fallen onto. The idea of pursuing certain 'career' can come out of envy of either another person's life style or something that is in-born with which if you ask that person why he or she has chosen that career you will told; "I do not know" or I just like it. At times "career" is hereditable where within the family thread and can be passed-on from one generation to another in the same family. You can find most of the family members or all of them work in the health delivery system or are in security, etc. It is also common with sport where we can find members of the same family in the same sporting activity at times to an extent of having more than one in the same team or club. It is interesting to note that one's basis of career has a bearing on his or her work performance.

(If you allow someone to plan your life you end-up blaming an innocent person for your poor planning or lack of it. (Sir Francis Mutimuri)

WORK PERFOMANCE VERSUS CAREER

When we execute our day to day duties at our work stations we draw attention in the form of negative or positive comments from those who become recipients of our work. This is common, especially, with those that work with the public. If your work is not your chosen career; your performance will always sell you out as no amount of training will change you.

Those that will have fallen for high perks or joined an organization as a result of laziness will have their heart and work always disengaged and complaints will always fly in their face. Interestingly; those whose work is their career are easy to train and ready volunteers in the time of need.

Your career should always be in line with your qualifications so that most of the jobs you do will be done from heart. Your 'curriculum vitae' should reflect and be indicative of your career through a flow of the same jobs related from one to another. You will; presumably, not be the right candidate if there is no smooth flow of related history of work when your prospective employer will look at your 'curriculum vitae' and see that there is no uniformity of experience whereby, you jumped from one unrelated work to another, thereby becoming a jack-of-of-all-trade like for example:- You are applying for a 'Farm Manager's post after you have moved from 'Mineral Exports Executive', to a 'Builder' and to 'Production Manager' at a radio manufacturing company, before joining the 'Police Force dog section'. You can see how quiet confusing it is. However, although not so common; depending on the seniority of the job, such dynamism can work a miracle for you as someone experienced in various sectors of economy although it is by far synonymous with a "chosen career".

CHAPTER 2

RECRUITMENT PROCESS

The term "recruitment" refers to the first stages in the process leading to the filling of a vacancy which arises (1) due to the creation of a new post, or (2) Because the present holder of it is leaving the employ of the organization or a section or department of it. At the heart of a successful staff is the selection of good workforce. The performance level of an average worker and that of the top worker are quite different.

For **any** manager – regardless of the technical aspects of the particular post, or the size or range of activities of the employing organization – a capable loyal team of staff is of **utmost importance.** Without that a manager cannot expect his or her department or section or business to operate smoothly and efficiently. No matter how automated an organization or part of it under a manager's control may be. The output of it will ultimately be achieved through the efforts of **people** – the manager's subordinates. Machines, materials and even premises can be replaced, but it is not at all easy to replace reliable hard working staff.

It is therefore vital that considerable attention is paid to the selection and recruitment of the **right** personnel. Equal consideration must be paid to the training of those people, and to their welfare, and to their motivation so that they will work well, willingly to some extent that they will be self-motivated and sufficiently content in the employment of the organization to stay with it. The need for – and the importance of – motivation were discussed in the preceding section, but the last point must be emphasized here, because the time, effort and expense involved in recruiting and training good personnel – and particularly perform well are considerable.

Large organization usually have personnel department – headed by a personnel manager – separate from the line or operating department. Such a department is responsible for dealing with many matters and problems relating to personnel throughout the organization: their conditions of work, welfare, recruitment, training, promotion, the maintenance of personnel records, etc. In smaller businesses it will be the owner or a senior manager, perhaps assisted by a clerk, who will responsible for such "personnel matters" Whatever the situation in a particular organization, a manager must be always deeply interested in matters concerning his personnel.

INTERNAL RECRUITMENT

This is the process of filling a vacancy by a person already employed by the organization; be it business or nonprofit organization. This may involve the promoting of a person currently working in the section or department or at another branch. Some organizations conduct active policies of internal promotion, the advantages of which can include:-

> Personnel who are aware that promotion is the reward of hard work and loyalty are motivated to learn and do more, and that leads to greater job satisfaction.

> The abilities and the potential of candidates for transfer and/or promotion might already be known to the manager, but if he (or the personnel department) can call for reports from the candidates' team leaders or supervisors, etc.

> Those promoted or transferred will have knowledge about the organization and possible about the work to be performed (especially if they have been given the opportunity to prepare for promotion) and so the induction and training process may be shorter.

EXTERNAL RECRUITMENT

There are also many **external** sources from which applicants can be drawn, and each one may produce the type of person for which a manager is looking. Here are examples:-

> Personnel recommendations or introductions from existing personnel often produce excellent personnel.

- Local employment agencies, government run or privately run, or personnel bureaux may supply staff. Some privately owned organizations specialize in location and selecting staff for specific posts or professions.

- Advertisements in national and/or local newspapers, either in classified "situation vacancies" or "appointments" columns, or by using lager, more expensive display advertisements.

- Advertisements in the trade journals or magazines of professional bodies; many of the later maintain registers of members and/or students seeking positions within the profession.

JOB DISCRIPTIONS

Before advertising a vacancy, the manager (perhaps with the aid of personnel department staff) should prepare a **job description** which, as its name implies, describes the job to be performed. It will briefly describe the tasks and duties involved in the job, the environment in which successful candidates will work, i.e, shop showroom, office, etc, or whether they will be required to work without supervision as managers, team leaders or as travelers. Details of such matters as hours of work, overtime, unsociable hours, holidays, sick leave, etc, will be stated in brief form, with details of salary, overtime rates, bonuses, commission and fringe benefits. The latter may include a pension scheme, sickness benefits and, if applicable – car allowance and the general expenses that may be incurred in the execution of duties involved.

IMPLOYEE SPECIFICATION

Having described the job to be performed, consideration must next be given by the manager to the "personal" qualities essential in, or which are desirable in the person(s) whom it is hoped to be found to perform the job concerned. Suitable personal qualities sought can and do vary considerably between posts, but they should be set down for each post in an **employee specification.**

Such a document should concentrate on the following categories of personal qualities, but according to *Susan Hamond's Business Studies* and in support thereof that will not necessarily include each quality in each category:-

- ➢ **Physical qualities,** such as upper and lower age limits, fluency of speech, eye sight, hearing, handwriting, dexterity (important in demonstrations of machines, for example), etc

- ➢ **Mental qualities,** such as intelligence, the ability to analyze, the ability to make decisions, mental alertness, the ability to use initiative and so on.

- ➢ **Skills or talents;** some posts require personnel with mechanical aptitude, others require a skill, e.g a salesman might have to demonstrate an appliance such as a washing machine, or timer on a cooker, or a motor vehicle, or a new type of video recorder or player, or performance of detergents, and so on.

- **Qualifications** are what will top their list of expectations. The prospective employer will want to see either they are derived from education, training or from hands-on (practical) experience. Experience with similar products may be most useful. According to CPM Training Manual Volume One *Page 4* on *Goods and Services* and in support thereof, please **note** that Goods and or Services are all products.

- **Personality and temperament,** requirements vary greatly; some posts call for bright, pleasing, enthusiastic and personality; the later in particular is an essential quality in some posts. The ability to work alone without constant supervision will be looked at by most recruiting officers.

Of note, is that whenever possible the job description and employee specification should be available **before** a vacancy arises, so steps can be taken to attract suitable applicants without delay. Special emphasis will be directed toward attracting **suitable candidates** and stimulating them to apply as it will be of no value wasting time and money attracting and dealing with numerous unsuitable applicants. On the other hand, if there are only a few applicants there may be no real choice and costs incurred would be a waste while the whole process and time incurred become a wasted start.

ADVERTISING FOR PERSONNEL

Some advertisements for personnel are left purposely "vague" in their content. They are phrased in such a manner that potential applicants who believe that they have the necessary qualifications for the post, will be encouraged to apply, whilst those who have no such confidence in their abilities will be deterred from responding. Here is an example in fig 1/1.

Fig 1/1: A specimen advertisement for personnel

An advertisement that is shown in Fig 1/1 would be fully understood by a professional marketer, who – even if presently employed would be tempted to go for a new opportunity which could supplement his income in the first instance and, if lucrative, become his main employment. Many marketers accept such jobs and work hard and successfully at them until another "vague" advertisement announces indirectly "A speciality marketer is required, must have own transport, high rates of commission might be paid but only on sales made" thus if the sales made totaled $1000, 15% commission might be paid plus 5% expenses. This ensures that the employer incurs selling expenses only after sales are actually made.

Generally speaking, however, managers design advertisements which state clearly the type(s) of person(s) required, the salary rage and what the post holder(s) will be required to do, where they will be expected to work, and what other benefits and prospects can be expected, currently and in the future, Finally the name and address of the person or the organization to which applications must be forwarded, or an advertisement voucher must be stated. Alternatively a name and telephone number may be given so that those interested may telephone for more information and, possibly to arrange for an interview.

In many cases an application form is sent to each applicant, for completion and return, Employment application forms must be carefully designed to ensure that:-

- Not only is the essential information about applicants obtained (and it important that "blank spaces of appropriate sizes are provided in which the required information can be written) but also

- That it is provided in the correct sequence to assist the selection process.

There may, of course, need to be deferent forms for deferent types of posts. In addition, it may be necessary to send out, with the blank application forms, sheets containing further information about the organization or about the post (such as the copy of the job description) and, particularly if the vacancy is in a deferent town or even country, information about the locality in which the successful applicant will work.

SELECTION

The selection process follows on from the recruitment process once applications start being received, e.g, by email, or by post. The first step is to compare the information provided by applicants with the personal characteristics in the employee specification, and to select applicants considered suitable for the post(s). Those selected will then be invited to attend interview(s)

A review of the most successful applicant in any organization is likely to reveal a good number of those who are introverted, mild-minded, slovenly and far from energetic. Alternatively the successful ones will include applicants who are articulate, well groomed, mean and well mannered.

CHAPTER 3

CURRICULUM VITAE (CV)

HOW TO PREPARE CURRICULUM VITAE

I will, in most parts, refer to Curriculum Vitae as **"CV"** as it is commonly known. A **"CV"** is your "torch bearer", your "go-between" which in all circumstances must not fail you. It must stimulate and arouse 'interest' of the recipient who is always your "prospective employer". As a good 'representative' must always do; it should portray you in a good picture and must not lack as it gives a true reflection of 'who you are'. It must, ultimately, see you being called for an Interview.

Preparation and Delivery

Just imagine; you definitely want a job that was advertised and instead of sending someone to go and lobby on your behalf you have sent a **"CV"** to do it. The moment your "CV" enters the hands of the 'recruiting officer(s)' – it must make them develop "love at first sight" by just looking at it. Its front cover must be 'eye catching' with a 'professional look'. It does not mean you must decorate it. Remember, "anything too much is wrong", therefore, your border-lines on the front page if you are to put any must be moderate and not too stylish so as to avoid making it look funny and unprofessional. The number of "CV" pages need not be too many or bulky; may be limited to plus or minus 3 and not exceeding 5. If your pages are bulky; it is common that most prospective employers get bored of reading it and will at the same time; be discouraged from going through it page-by-page to the end. Also make sure that you do not seal the envelope containing your CV; you may only tuck when closing it. Most recruiting officers prefer opening unsealed envelopes first and they have a tendency of ignoring sealed ones, however, I say this without painting them all with one brush. Some of them have can easily place them somewhere, where they may end up gathering dust or worse still take them into the bin. That can only be countered by making sure that **your envelope is not sealed and that the number of pages are not bulky.** However, all necessary supporting documents like certificates and reference letters must be attached to the CV. You are advised to attach all copies together in uniformity manner since, in most cases; 'loose' pages would end up missing.

There are three ways in which an "Application Letter for employment" can be delivered. Normally; every advertised vacancy sets out, (especially at the most bottom part) the way, which, recruiting officers would want applications delivered to them. The three ways are by (1) 'Hand delivery', (2) 'Post Office,' and (3) 'Email'. Email delivery system is commonly used because it is so fast and its costs are relatively low. Email system is so easy to work with, even recruiting officers will find it easy to open and start reading your CV by matter of a click on their computer. It is always easy also to file "soft copies" than "hard copies". In addition – email system is now commonly used when applying for jobs abroad.

To be more precise:- 'Soft Copies' are computer generated and are deliverable by means of 'email', and 'Hard Copies' are paper-work generated, meaning, they are the ones with which we deliver by hand or through "Post Offices" in envelops. This delivery system requires a lot of smartness on the preparation, handling and delivery.

Your envelope and copies enclosed inside must be neat and tidy, meaning, there should be nowhere cancelled or hand written except your 'Application/Covering' letter which in most cases recruiting officers would be happy to see your 'hand-writing' and 'grammar' which is **not** computer assisted. However, in most cases, the design and lay-out of a CV either 'hard copies' or 'soft copies' remains the same.

Design and Layout

The design and layout of a CV can defer country by country or region and you are advised to follow what you are used to in your country or region, however, contents are the same. Therefore, there is an example of a standard CV below to help beginners with a clue on how it is written. In most cases; whichever professional way you design it, would make it acceptable because what comes first and follows next and comes last remains the same. Also, not overlooking the fact that, like "culture", "technology" is also dynamic due to the advancement of civilization, thus, we must follow suit on generational changes and technological advancement.

The following is an example of a **Standard Curriculum Vitae (CV)**

CURRICULUM VITAE

FOR
....

Physical Address
....
....
Postal Address
....
....
Cell:..............................

PERSONAL DETAILS

First Name	:..
Surname	:..
Sex	:..
Date	:..
Marital Status	:..
Nationality	:..

Languages   : ....

Email Address   : ....

Hobbies   : ....

Interests   : ....

ACADEMIC QUALIFICATIONS

Level attained : ....

Subjects Passed : ....

1. ....

2. ....

3. ....

4. ....

5. ....

<u>**PROFESSIONAL QUALIFICATIONS**</u>

1. ....

2. ....

3. ....

4. ....

5. ....

WORKING HISTORY and EXPERIENCE (see table below)

COMPANY	POSITION HELD	PERIOD	DURATION
BELONAONE INVESTMENT (Pvt) LTD	Sales and Marketing Director -reporting to the Managing Director	2012-2020	7 years
THREE STAR GLOBAL TRADING (Pty) LTD	Export Sales Executive -reporting to The General Manager	2009-2012	3 years
EDMUND IMPORT/EXPORT AGENCY (LLC)	Warehouse Supervisor -reporting the Warehouse Manager	2005-2009	4 years

CURRENT EMPLOYMENT

Employer : BELONAONE INVESTMENT (Pvt) LTD

Position : Marketing Director

Period : From 13 March 2019 to date

OTHER ACTIVITIES

- ....
  ....
  ....

- ....
  ....
  ....

- ....
  ....
  ....

- **DIPLOMA IN SALES and MARKETING MANAGEMENT**
- Topics Covered
- ....
....
....
....
....
....
....
....

- **DIPLOMA IN INTERNATIONAL TRADE**
- Topics Covered
- ....
....
....
....
....
....
....
....

- **CERTIFICATE IN MARKETING**
- Topics Covered
- ....
....
....
....
....
....
....
....
....

- **CERTIFICATE IN SALES REPRESENTATIVE**

- Topics Covered

- ....
  ....
  ....
  ....
  ....
  ....
  ....

- **CERTIFICATE IN FIRST AID, BASIC HEALTH AND HYGIENE**

- Topics Covered

- ....
  ....
  ....
  ....
  ....
  ....
  ....
  ....
  ....

- **Next Of Kin**

- Full Name :..

- Contact Details

- Telephone :...

- Physical Address..

- **References**

- Full Name..

- Contact Details..

- 2) Full Name...

- Contact Details..

- 3) Full name...

- Contact Details..

Your "CV" must be constructed in such a way that will indicate a smooth flow of events as indicated above. Everything must tally with what in either of the two. A "CV" alone without an "Application/Covering Letter" is not enough.

CHAPTER 4

APPLICATION LETTER

As a prospective candidate you indicate your strengths, experiences and wishes (how you expect to contribute to the growth of that company/business once an opportunity is granted). Your salutation must be professional and indicative of some moral values. You must never use slang, abbreviations only in your CV or application letter. Do not become overzealous by addressing one as 'Boss' or desperate by becoming too persuasive or obsessed by indicating as if the job is already yours. Nowadays; all addresses must be one sided to your far left side with the recipient's address on top followed by yours. Make sure that the information in your CV and Application letter will tally. Your "application letter" will play the role of a messenger for you.

The following is how an application letter should look like:-

Three Star Global Trading (Pty) LTD

20003 Lorwaneng

Mahikeng

Northwest Province

South Africa

24/02/2020

11263 D Overspill

Epworth

Harare

Zimbabwe

The Human Resources Manager

Ref:-APPLICATION FOR EXPORT SALES EXECUTIVE

I have seen your vacancy advertisement in the Sunday Mail Newspaper of 23 February 2020 and am happy to inform you through this application that I am very much interested in the employ of your esteemed company. I have 14 years hands-on experience in the field of the job advertised and will not hesitate to take the offer when this application is considered.

I have a Diploma in International Trade (UK) where I specialized in Import-Export Sales and am a full member of Wade World Trade Organisation (WWTO) with membership number ZW/0112/M9. I also have a prestigious Diploma in Sales and Marketing Management which I did with a British based College of Professional Management (CPM). In addition to above I have managed to obtain the following local Certificates in Marketing, Sales Representative and First Aid. Socially I am currently the chairman of Crime Consultative Committee of Zimbabwe Republic Police of Chegutu District Area 4 and I have a valid Police Clearance Certificate. Once given an opportunity I am fully prepared to take your company to some other stage of development by expanding its market share throughout the world and you will always enjoy my workmanship enriched over so many years of working experience. My recruitment with your organization will prove to be an excellent add-on to your sustainable development and expansion of your market share to some exciting levels.

Hopefully, you will have pleasure working with me and will be very much happy if you are going to consider my application. Looking forward to hearing from you, hopefully, with a view to taking things a stage forward.

Yours Faithfully

....

Edmund Mutimuri

You should make sure that your application letter fits on one page and that it is structured well enough to impress your prospective employer.

CHAPTER 5

The INTERVIEW and PROCEDURES

Definition

The initial meeting and discussion for employment vacancy by and between the Candidate and the Interviewer is called the '**Interview**'

This is the time when you should be able sell and market yourself by presenting yourself and your papers well before, during and after the interview. Therefore, your Curriculum Vitae (CV) presentation is going to be your starting point and a tool to market yourself in your absence. Thus, as you send your CV to your prospective employer it has to be an excellent representative of yours and must force your interviewer to visualize you in the eye of his mind as the right prospect for employment and suitable for listing.

APPLICATION RATING PROCEDURES

For a business to operate smoothly and efficiently it is of utmost importance that it recruits loyal personnel, thereby, ensuring that is has a capable team of staff regardless of its size or its 'technical' aspect of particular post. **One can replace premises, materials and machines but it is not easy at all to replace reliable, honest and hardworking staff**. Increasing number of companies now give formal tests to applicants, however, it would depend on the type of the job on offer. Although test scores are only one information element in a scheme that includes personal characteristics, references, past employment history and interviewee relations, they are weighed quite heavily by some companies.

Recruitment procedures should lead to the development of more applicants than jobs, and the company's task is to select better applicants.

Selection procedures vary in elaborateness from a single informal interview to highly detailed testing and interviewing, not only to the man but maybe extended to the wife also.

It is not simple with the choice of an appropriate battery of tests. Standard tests are available to measure intelligence, interests, aptitude, personal adjustment, personality, characteristics and social intelligence where upon personal reactions may also be put to test, eg, by cracking a joke.

There are also tailor made tests for special situations. These tests vary considerably, however, they are prone to manipulation by applicants, like, and for example, a man can fake a low IQ if he thinks this is desirable. He can also spot red-herring questions such as "do you prefer tennis or reading". Take care of the following set of rules that may be laid down for the job applicant who takes company psychology test:-

1)-Show that you like things as they are;

2)-Give the most conventional answer and-

3)-indicate that you never worry and-

4)-Deny any taste for books and music

CHAPTER 6

PERCENTAGE OF RESPONDANTS RATING

According to *Stephen Dank's Business Studies 3rd addition* one should bear in mind that the following will be used also as performance rating, measured in percentages on various disciplines by the interviewer at the end of the interview. For example:-

- Communication skills 40%

- Personality 31%

- Determination 30%

- Intelligence 27%

- Motivation/Self-motivation 52%

- Product knowledge 60%

- Educational background 65%

- Confidence 82%

- Appearance 12%

- Resilience and tenacity 47%

- Business sense 45%
- Integrity 19%
- Ambition 70%
- Acceptability/likeability 15%
- Empathy 47%
- Initiative 75%
- Self-discipline 15%
- Confidence 60%
- Adaptability 72%
- Persuasiveness 6%

It must be noted that employment application forms may be carefully designed to ensure that:-

- Not only is the **essential information** about applicants obtained; but also that "blank spaces" of appropriate sizes are provided in which the required information can be written and also;

- That it is provided in the **best sequence** to assist the selection process.

CHAPTER 7

CONTINUATION OF INTERVIEW PROCESSES and TIPS

SELECTION

The selection process forms the background and follows on from the recruitment process once applications start being received. Comparison of the information provided by applicants comes first and a shortlist comes about as a result of scrutiny made from personal characteristics. Those selected will then be invited to attend interviews.

EMPLOYMENT INTERVIEW

The initial meeting and discussion for employment vacancy by and between the Candidate and the Interviewer is called the '**Interview**'. Generally a number of candidates for a vacant post have to be interviewed, and so a 'series' of interviews will be held. They might all be held one day, or spread in 'sessions' of two or more over a number of days. The process of interviewing candidates for employment is a most important one, and so, proper attention must be paid to the planning and conduct of interview in a series.

AIMS OF INTERVIEW

- To enable the interviewer(s) to confirm information provided by the candidate, to obtain further information and, if necessary, to read and see originals of documents (testimonials from former employers, certificates/diplomas and degrees, school reports, etc.)

- To enable a candidate to obtain more information and about the organization and the job and the "terms and conditions of employment".

- To enable the interviewer(s) to compare more accurately each candidate's characteristics with those detailed in the employee specification and thus to assess the suitability of the candidate for the post.

- To enable the interviewer(s) – at the end of the session of interviews – to decide which is the most suitable candidate for the job and to encourage that candidate to join the organization.

The session(s) of interviews might not achieve either or both of the objectives in the final paragraph. It is possible that none of the candidates is considered suitable, in which case those applications previously "rejected" might have to be looked at again. On the other hand, two or more candidates might be considered similarly, or equally suitable in which case they might be "short-listed" and asked to attend a second interview. It might be that, in any case, the candidate considered to be the most suitable might decline (for any of a variety of deferent reasons) to accept the position when offered. Thus, with this in mind, it is folly and senseless for the interviewer or prospective employer to always think that once a vacant becomes available it will be filled at once with ease.

PRELIMINARY INTERVIEW PROCEDURE

In large companies, and particularly when a number of candidates are to be recruited at one time, "preliminary" interviews might be conducted by personnel department staff, using the *"job descriptions"* and *"the employee specifications"* prepared by, or in conjunction with the department manager as their guide. Such a practice – is often called "screening" can save the manager personally having to waste time interviewing numerous applicants, many of whom may totally be unsuitable, or who are undesirable for employment. It might be also necessary for any of the department manager to attend such "screening" **interview**.

The 'qualities' looked for during these preliminary interviews will, of course, depend on the posts to be filled; the type of the job to be performed , how senior the posts are, what supervision – if any-will be provided, sector and so on.

Questionnaire Forms may be used and once completed may then be attached to the applicant's original application letter or completed application form be forwarded to the department manager for assessment. The manager will grade the application letters in accordance with interviewer's code and with the applicants' own answers to the questions. Some applications will probably be rejected at once, but the department manager can probably decide to interview personally some of those who made applications and "passed" the preliminary interview.

PLANNING and PREPARING FOR INTERVIEW

The proper preparation and planning for interviews are both essential for satisfactory and productive results, therefore, an interviewee must know the following:-

- It must be accepted that some candidates may be nervous or shy during an interview and, particularly if they have not attended an interview before, may be apprehensive about the whole affair. Therefore, if the interviewer is to be able to assess such candidates, he or she must put them at ease as soon as possible. For instance, if the candidates have to wait before being interviewed, the room in which they will have to wait should be pleasant, quite and comfortable; and the receptionist or secretary who will meet them should be asked to treat them in a welcoming and friendly fashion – certainly **not disinterestedly or off-handedly.**

- An attempt should be made to break any barriers as soon as the candidate enters the room; for example by the interviewer(s) standing up, making a pleasant or friendly remark, and even by coming out from behind the desk. Prior arrangements should be made to ensure that there are no interruptions such as telephones or intercoms ringing or visitors entering the room, cell phones must be switched off. An interviewee must be cool and able to smile.

- A candidate must avoid any form of wayward behaviour as such may cause you to be dismissed before the interview conversation begins because any continuation will be a waste of time.

- Dark shades/Sun glasses must be removed except those that may have been prescribed or recommended by a doctor. In this case you must politely indicate to the interviewer of any such recommendations from the doctor. For example; you may say it like this: *I am sorry sir for any inconvenience, my glasses are a recommendation from the doctor that I must put them on always, I do not know if you can allow me to?* This way, you will always find the "Yes" answer.

- You must dress smartly and accordingly.

- An interviewer might be offended if an interviewee is too "pushy", therefore, care is required, particularly if the interviewer is hesitant or evasive about telling you. Being too "pushy" can be indicated verbally or through body signs, so tact is essential to ensure that you never do it either way.

- Even if you are personally known to the Interviewer, do not be obsessed and think that the job is already yours. Your performance should always be at par.

CHAPTER 8

TECHNIQUES and PREPERATION TIPS (Starting from home)

Excellent performances on your interview, a well put up CV and an application letter that commensurate with the given Job Description are contributing factors that will see you getting short listed and ultimately invited for that job.

In support of *P Allen's Selling Management and Practice*, prospective interviewees are strongly advised to ensure that they take a birth first before setting their foot off for an interview and make sure their hair is done properly **but not** tinted.

- LADIES - Depending with the type of job you are vying for, make sure your hair is done in such a way that will suit the intended job. Avoid tying your hair with anything flashy. Your make-up must always be simple and not too visible or flashy in order to avoid looking funny in front of the interviewer. At least you may wear a single necklace and a wristband not a bunch of them. In the case of wristbands make sure the one you put on is fashionable. And always avoid wearing wristbands which shows the church that you go to unless you know very well that the one that is going to interview you is of the same church or fellowship with you {this applies to both sex male and female} otherwise never put any as most interviewers are skeptical about them. Depending with the country and type of job applied for, ladies may put-on trousers **and not** Short Trousers. Over and above they should dress formally except in special circumstances like with fashionable jobs as explained above.

- MEN – make sure your hair is cut short and reasonably shaped. With men, plain cuts are mostly preferred as fancy cuts will always portray you in a bad picture. Hair cut prepared for an interview must always be short and simple. Moustache must also be short and in simple style. Men must always avoid wearing necklaces and wristbands when they are going for interview. Locks must also be avoided as most interviewers (depending with the country) are skeptical about them. Although it is a human right they will not serve the purpose if they make you lose the job. Make sure you brush your teeth (both sex) before leaving home to avoid any smell during interview process.

DRESSING IN GENERAL

It is always advisable that one dresses formally and avoids wearing of any hat, three quarter trousers and/or mini-skirt. Avoid also wearing of flashy clothes. However, with ladies ear rings are recommended as long as they match the clothes put on. Tight and short **and not** mini-dresses in some cases with ladies can be recommended especially when the job applied for is more to do with fashion. Ladies may wear fashionable clothes in this case; otherwise avoid them at all with some other jobs. However, culture defers from one country to another, in some countries like Arab states dress code is the same so this may not apply.

PERFUMES

Care must be taken with the spray of perfumes as you may not know whether or not your interviewer is allergic to it. Yes it works perfectly well to improve your confidence but care must be taken to ensure that you do not apply too much of it as some may not like the fragrance or are allergic to it, so you are best advised to balance between the two. Take your time to prepare before leaving home as any rush may lead to unwarranted mistakes.

PRAYER

This must be the integral part of your preparation as above all things everything is made possible by the Almighty God the father of us all. It will never be complete unless it is sufficiently enough for completion and that sufficiency is made complete by prayer. Kindly **NOTE** – the word "**sufficiency**" is derived from the greek word "**hikanotes**" meaning competence; being qualified enough to be able, and being "up-to-the-task", *(You can read 2 Corinthians 3 vs 5 and John 14 vs 13-14). Remember, you may not be the only* *person being interviewed for that job so the cover of the Holy Spirit is necessary for your preparedness. Your preparation can be made sufficient enough for competence through divine prayer. Even apostle Paul said in Philipians 4 vs 13, "I can do all things through Christ who strengthens me".*

TIME MANAGEMENT

At this stage your time management is of paramount importance. Make sure you leave a lee-way time for any possible delays on your way to the interview. (Lee-way time in this case is any extra time provided to cater for any possible delays made on way)

1)-If you are to hitchhike, make sure you have enough extra time as you may not know when you are going to get delayed on the way or when you are going to catch the next transport.

2)-If you are to go footing, make sure at no time shall you ever run or walk too fast so as to avoid sweating, something which would end up discrediting you and destroying your confidence because of the odor that may be coming out of your body.

3)-If you are to use own vehicle make sure you have made enough checks and that you have enough fuel to take you exactly to where the interview is going to take place. Give yourself some lee-way time for possible delays like getting yourself hogged in-between other slow moving vehicles.

4)-If you are to use local airplane make sure you buy your air ticket well in advance and that you arrive at the airport well in time to ensure that you never miss your first flight. Make sure you will be able to find a vehicle to take you to the intended destination well in time. The same applies when you are to travel to another country for the interview, however, in addition to above is that you are well advised to reach the country and point of destination a day or two before, for you to familiarize yourself with people and the surrounding area of your intended destination.

In this case you are also advised to personally visit the premise that the interview is to be conducted. However, extreme care and caution must be exercised to avoid infringing your next official visit.

On the actual day of interview you are duly advised to ensure that you arrive at the exact place of interview not too early and **not** later than 10 minutes before starting time. Be advised not to arrive too early in order to avoid ending up sleeping inside the premise where the interview is to take place. At most, plus or minus 30 minutes early is okay.

CHAPTER 9

FROM THE MAIN GATE TO THE INTERVIEW ROOM

Suppose the premise is fenced or has a Dura wall and you are now by the gate. Most occasionally you will find the gate manned by a security guard or you will be served through the intercom or its free entrance. The guard may need to know the purpose/reason of your visit. Do not hesitate to let him/her know that you are short listed and/or invited for interview on that particular date and time. Avoid any form of quarreling with him and if any misunderstanding arises then you should ask him to refer the matter to the responsible official inside without wasting time. If you are to be served through the intercom make sure that you do not stammer or sound confused. You must politely introduce yourself first and then go straight to the point by stressing out the reason behind your visit. Any form of quarrelling at the gate especially with the guard will only serve to embarrass and destroy your confidence and morally which at this time must be maintained at every cost.

INSIDE THE COMPLEX

Now that you have entered inside the complex and you are heading toward where others are seated or to any point where you may have been instructed to. You are well advised **never** to shortcut your way at any point as you walk to the recommended point. Always use the designated pathway or pavement. If you are driving make sure you follow the designated way and parking space. Avoid restricted areas like "reserved parking space" when inside. Remember to switch off your alarm before you leave your car as it may end up forcing you to switch it off in a hast and in the middle of an interview something which will only embarrass you and obstruct the smooth flow of interview process which at no time need not be disturbed.

One may lose all morally and confidence facing the embarrassment of being called upon only to be warned that where you are moving on is a restricted area. When the Interviewer over-hears you getting warned, then, he/she may have a bad feeling about you before you even enter the interview room. Guard your manners jealously while inside the premise. Never peep inside any of the rooms, run, or laugh aloud. Try to find where the bin is and avoid littering. Make sure you respond to the call of nature and visit the toilet before you enter the interview room. Avoid messing the toilet as it may be noticed that it's you who did that. Again you are advised **never** to take pictures inside.

Now that you are about to get inside the offices and are left with about ten minutes, it's now time to tidy yourself and put things to order, eg – removing dust on yourself if any and shining your shoes, attend your hair and make-up, etc. It is your last chance to sort out your papers as well. After all this you can wait and pay attention to be called inside. When a waiting room is provided and you cannot tidy yourself in-there maybe because of the presence of other people inside then you can take advantage and do it in the toilet. Wait outside until you are called in.

AT THE DOOR

Take care as your behaviour while outside has effect inside. When you are called in, be gentle and do not rush to the door. If you find the door closed make sure you leave it closed and if you find it open leave it open as you go inside. However, you might be given an instruction by the room occupants to either leave it open or closed; therefore, you have to follow that instruction. Always avoid banging it either to the door frame or to the wall as you close or open it.

Remember, at no time shall you remove your shoes or leave them by the doormat even if they are dirty or when you no longer feel comfortable of them. With some cultures across the globe it is taboo to do that. You must have a handkerchief, a small towel or any clean whipping clothe ready with you in case mucus oozes out through your nose at any time during the course of your interview process. Oozing of mucus and puffing are calls of nature that disturbs but can be prevented. Mucus is by nature so stubborn especially in cold weathers and mores so with people that are not used to cold weathers and/or when you are flue infected. Avoid any possible embarrassment while inside.

SOME TIPS AND AREAS THAT REQUIRE SPECIAL ATTENTION

I. -With men, if you hurry up too much, there is a tendency with trousers getting tucked in the socks.

II. -With ladies, there is a tendency with dresses and/or skirts turning up as you stand up from a seating position.

III. -Check your zips also especially after leaving the toilet.

IV. -Clothes are in habit of getting swallowed in-between the buttocks as we stand up, so, care must be taken and, so, therefore, check just after standing up.

There are still so many other things that you may think about and some of them need not attended to while you are now at the door but back home or during waiting time. Make sure you have done all the checks to yourself and documents before you enter as not doing so may end-up tarnishing your image as it will indicate that you are not organized. That's why arriving well in time before commencement of interview is recommended.

After you have gently knocked and heard a "come in" instruction you open the door (not hastily but swiftly) and then walk straight inside showing enough energy as an indication of ability to do the work once you become successful.

CHAPTER 10

INSIDE THE OFFICE(S)

In addition, this is the most important time as room occupants or interviewer may have their first sight of you as you approach them for the first time. Remember in life, once someone **looks down upon you at his/her first sight of you as you approach** then your chances of success become slim with that person. **Therefore, you must make sure that you have done all you can to impress your hosts at first sight.**

After you have been answered "come in" you may now walk straight ahead to where you are instructed to by either the first attendant who may happen to be the secretary, receptionist, the interviewer or anyone of authority. Be careful while you walk inside, mind your steps and neither stumble over anything nor drag your feet.

Now you need to be in the right frame of mind and sober. At this time you must forget about anything which may have once upset or embarrassed you on your way to the interview.

Politely greet whoever attends to you, however, with a smile on your face and take care not to greet the same person twice. Remember, it is by nature that 'smiling' can improve your own confidence and can boost or amend relations. Bearing in mind that your first interview began the moment you entered the premise, so, you are advised to continuously behave well throughout the whole process. Also bearing in mind that culture is dynamic and differs from one country to another, so as character do from one person to another, therefore, with this in mind you are obliged to expect and accept all responses and act accordingly.

The first attendant may not be interested or may just be reluctant to handshake you so you are advised to quickly use your judgment, adaptability and wisdom to see whether he is interested or not. And if he wants a handshake you must, therefore, with a smile in the face, respond back by fully stretching-out your hand and handshake him/her while you avoid handshaking with the end of your finger-tips. When he is not interested in handshaking, just don't mind about it but follow any given instructions.

AT THE DESK

Be very attentive as you approach the interviewer's desk. Remember to show that you are quite energetic and up-to-task. Some interviewers, although not many, may not be interested in the handshaking fashion and may only give an instruction to get you seated by show of hand signal. Don't be annoyed by that but just follow the given instruction. Normally the interviewer should stand up and handshake the interviewee first before telling him to seat down. Remember never to seat down before you are asked to, and, when doing so you must never pull the chair. At this point you should stand by the side of the chair and wait for a 'seat down' instruction. The system follows that you will now be asked to seat down and is when you gently lift up the chair without making noise while you avoid pulling it off especially when the chair was left leaning against the desk. However, you should adjust it to allow yourself to comfortably seat on it without making unnecessary movements.

SOME NECESSARY TIPS

When you are getting seated make sure you gently seat without falling yourself on the chair and:-

I. - do not put your hands or let them rest on top of the desk; instead, you should either fold them by your chest or put them on top of your thighs.

II. - with ladies who are breast-feeding or those that have large breasts you may avoid folding your hands by your chest, therefore, you may only put them on top of your thighs.

III. - do not let your legs encroach and/or get into contact with that of your interviewer's legs under the desk.

IV. - Chewing a mint sweet few moments before you are called in can play a trick here by improving the smell from your mouth, however, you must avoid chewing anything from the time you enter into the office and during the time of interview process. When you happen to cough or yawning make sure you have your mouth covered while looking aside or down.

V. - avoid unnecessary gestures like looking around the room even if you are left alone as during these days with modern technology there might be someone elsewhere watching you through a CCTV. Therefore, you should never unnecessarily touch or stand up for anything.

VI. - avoid interjecting your interviewer or asking questions as if you the interviewer.

VII. - ensure that you always talk with your face raised up

VIII. - listen carefully to each and every question before you provide an answer.

IX. - Remember most people, especially interviewers are very skeptical about tattoos especially in Africa and most other parts of the World, so, you may have them with all reasoning and care for the future otherwise never.

X. -Handing of papers must be done with both hands

XI. -your answer should be straight to the point and you must answer only that which is asked

XII. -Avoid crossing your legs when you are seated

CHAPTER 11

PSYCHOLOGICAL TESTS FOR CANDIDATES SELECTION

Although success at the interview is always an important determinant of selection, some companies employ supplementary techniques to provide a valid measure of potential. A number of large companies use psychological tests in this way. However care has to be taken when using these tests and a trained psychologist is needed to administer and interpret the results. Further, there are a number of criticisms which have been leveled at the tests.

I. - It is easy to cheat. The applicant, having an idea of the type of a person who is likely to be successful at the given task, does not respond truly but fakes the test in order to give a 'correct' profile. For example, in response to questions such as, "Who is of more value to society – the practical man or the thinker?" He answers "the practical man" no matter what his true convictions may be.

II. - Many tests measure interest rather than ability. The manager knows the interests of the successful candidates and uses tests to discover their level of intelligence and see if potential new recruits have similar interest patterns. The assumption here is that success on the given task can be predicted by the type of interests which a person has. This is unlikely as discovering a new *Lionel Messy* by measuring the interests of young footballers.

III. - Tests have been used to identify individual personality traits which may not be associated with success on the job. Factors such as how sociable, dominant, friendly and loyal a person is have been measured in order to predict how successful one is to be on the job. While some of these factors may be useful attributes for a candidate to posses. Mayer and Greenberg have shown that success can be reasonably accurately predicted once these characteristics are known. The ideal is a candidate who possesses a high degree of all the above factors. A high degree of empathy (an ability to feel as the other person feels) and ego drive (the need to be successful in a personal way) are usually associated with high performance on the job. Plenty of empathy but little ego drive means the candidate will be liked by those associated with his/her job. Finally, the candidate with little empathy and ego drive will be a complete failure.

THE USE OF NUETRAL QUESTIONS

Basic principle of good interviewing is to use neutral rather than leading questions. The question, 'Can you tell me about the training you received at your previous employer?' is likely to lead to rather different, less biased responds than 'I'm sure you learnt a lot from your courses, didn't you?' is more neutral than 'I'm sure you wouldn't have any problems dealing with the task I gave you, 'would you?

COMMONLY ASKED QUESTIONS AND INFORMATION REQUIRED

- -Can you tell us about yourself? – (This shall refer to who you are regarding education, personality, Character, Temperament, Life achievements, Interests and hobbies)

- -Give us a brief history about yourself – (This shall refer to work history and experience)

- -How many are you in your family and you are at which number? –(This shall be used to measure possible load in your life)

- -When given a chance, how do you thing you can develop this company? –(This shall be used to measure how **useless** in their company you shall be so you must be very careful here and use tact by showing that you are someone who is initiative and strategic for development but limited to the level of your intended employment)

- -Do you have any or chronic disease? – (Tact is essential here and avoid the obvious thing becoming obvious)

- *-What is your interest and hobby?* –(This shall be used to measure the possibility of **anything negative always happening** in line of your employment)

- *-Do you like travelling?* – (This question is normally asked when your intended job requires traveling and shall be used to see if your duties shall be properly executed)

- *-If you are married how many children and dependants do you have?* (This question shall be used to measure how much pressure and load you have. Tact must also be used here as any indication of too much pressure can lead your interviewer into thinking that you are more tempted to steal from the company or funny enough – this shall draw some lenience from the interviewer.)

- *-What is your favorite food?* (This question is normally used to clear some tense in the room as food matters are normally discussed with some smiles and jokes)

- *-Do you like learning?* (You must always indicate that you like leaning as any dislike thereof will portray you negatively and as a damn)

- *-What is your highest level of education?* (Your answer to this question must always tally with copies of certificates provided and you must be very honest here as **any exaggeration** thereof will always show on the execution of your duties)

- *-Can you work in a team?* (Failure to work in a team will always be approached with a big "NO", therefore, you will obviously not be appropriate for the job)

- *-Are both of your parents still alive?* (This question is normally asked in order to derive in-depth knowledge about yourself)

- *-What is your favorite sport?* (This question is also normally asked in order to derive in-depth knowledge about yourself)

- *-Do you have any allergy?* (This question is normally asked in order to derive in-depth knowledge about yourself)

- *-Who is your favorite musician?* (This question is normally asked in order to derive in-depth knowledge about yourself)

- *What is your expected salary?* (This question must always be answered with tact as any mishap will possibly put off your interviewer and lead him into thinking that you are not the appropriate person for the job. I suggest that you answer this question like this; "I think you are a fair employer who will pay me as the job commensurate". An answer given like this will not provide your interviewer with an exact figure which will without your knowledge offend your interviewer as your given figure might be too much or too little. If your expected salary is too much with them then you will not be their appropriate choice and again if your figure is too little it will be an indication of desperation. Desperation can never be an advantage as your possibility to stay on the job will always be doubted and portrayed as a possible waste of effort.)

The above commonly asked questions are used to measure the interviewee's aptitude, character, personality trait, temperaments and behaviour, so you must be very careful when answering such questions.

CHAPTER 12

The Interview Session (Interviewee versus Interviewer)

NOTE-I have not said 'when the interview process begins' but 'when the interview session begins' because the actual interview will have begun by the time you entered the premises. Remember also that I have once said, 'your behaviour outside the offices has influence inside'.

In addition, as I give special emphasis on the practical aspect of the interview process and to the effect that you have now come face to face with your interviewer or at times a panel comprising two or more of them, you must now put yourself at ease, remove all the fear and pay special attention. Remain focused and look straight into the eyes of the one talking to you so as to bolster your confidence and attention. You must have your cell phone switched off by this time to avoid obstruction of a smooth flow of the interview at any given point during the interview process.

There are some interviewers who are full of jokes. Make sure you will at no time laugh aloud or else never laugh at all, however, do not hesitate to share a smile. At times jokes are deliberately cracked in order to test the depth of how one would lose self control.

QUESTIONNAIRE FORM

You might be provided with an interview questionnaire form of which you must first carefully read and understand instructions provided therein before you start giving answers.

When answering questions whether written or verbal, you must avoid giving answers as "yes or no" only, instead, support your answers with a statement. For example:- let's say you are asked; 'are both of your parents still alive?' your answer should be 'yes they all still alive' or 'no my father passed away few years back and only my mother is still alive.'

During the interview process, you must never talk while facing or looking down or leaning your head/cheek in your palm. When given a chance to ask questions be mindful of what you ask. However, it is normal with jobs of higher positions to ask about your remuneration with due care and diligence. For example you may ask like this, 'How much should I expect to get paid?'

You may also be asked 'how much is you're your expected salary?' And in addition to my earlier explanation on this question on Chapter 8 paragraph 4, you don't have to give a direct answer, so you may answer like this; " I think you are a fair employer who will pay me as the job commensurate". By this you will have avoided mentioning the exact figure something which would have marred your success ability and put the whole process into waste.

However, an empty box might have been provided for you to fill in the Questionnaire Form where an exact figure has to be written

It is important to find out first before you come for the interview how much others is such employment are earning, therefore you must provide your figure like this; "the figure you will have found out about others in such employment is the one which you give like for example; +/- $800." If you have not done any investigation about your possible remuneration before then, you must add your minimum and maximum expected salary and then divide the answer by 2. For example; "$600 being your minimum plus $1000 being your maximum divided by 2 =$800. You will now write in the box your figure as +/-$800

If you provide your answer as is above, your figure will most likely be expected and moderate. The plus or minus addition to it will neutralize the idea of it becoming too much or too little since room for the possibility of it being increased or reduced from the given figure will always be a welcome development.

CHAPTER 13

SOME CONSIDERATIONS

Here are some areas that the interviewee must know about the interviewer's conduct and considerations. According to Lancaster, Geoffrey A, and David Jobber's *Sales Techniques and Management* and in support thereof I suggest that:-

Firstly - Most of the time spent interviewing has to be used to evaluate the candidates.

Secondly - part of the interview will be a task in order to insure the chosen applicant accepts the job on offer. The balance between evaluation and the given task is largely based upon judgment, and no hard and fast rules apply, but obviously the competitive situation and the strength of the candidate will be two factors which affect the decision.

Thirdly – Be advised that the interviewer must discreetly control the interview. A certain amount of time will be allocated to each candidate and it is the interviewer's responsibility to ensure that all salient dimensions of the candidate are covered, not only those about which the candidate wishes to talk about. Some of the earlier techniques, used in reverse, may be necessary to discourage the candidate from rumbling on. For example, the interviewer may look disinterested, or ask a few closed questions to discourage verbosity. Alternatively the interviewer can simply interrupt with 'That's fine. I think we are quite clear on that point now,' at an appropriate moment.

Finally - the interviewer will need to close the interview when sufficient information has been obtained. Usually the candidate is forewarned of this by the interviewer saying 'Okay, we have asked you about yourself, are there any questions you would like to ask me(us)?' At the end of the interview session the interviewer explains when the decision will be made and how it will be communicated to the candidate and then thanks him about the interview. They then both shake hands and the candidate is shown to the door.

When the interview is almost through, the interviewer is expected to ask you about any other questions that you may have or anything else you may want to know about the company. At this point you can then ask about when you can expect the interview results if the matter has been omitted earlier on. Care must be given to ensure that you do not ask awkward questions that may as a result tarnish a once successful interview. **Never** ask too many questions

Before an interview is brought to a close, the interviewer will want to make sure that all necessary questions have been asked and that all the candidate's questions have been answered.

When you may now want to leave the room, you swiftly stand up and gently return the chair to its position. You may then say 'thank you' before you turn back. Mind your steps again as you walk out.

Avoid shortcutting your way out through to the main gate. Leave the doors as you found them like when you came in. Do not hang around inside the premises; instead, go straight out to the main gate and leave.

When you get home do not be obsessed and want to phone back for interview results before their given time.

NOTE-Make sure, from there on, you remains contactable and available in case they may want to contact you either by phone, email or personal visit.

SHORT-LISTING AFTER THE FIRST INTERVIEW

There is a possibility of having two or more candidates that may be considered to be equally suitable for the same post while only one is required. It is then necessary to 'short list' those candidates and call them for second interviews before a final decision is made on who will be offered the post.

Depending on the types of posts, certain selection tests may be used to supplement – but not to replace – the selection interview. Some tests are fairly straightforward, such as work tests designed to check if a candidate is as skillful as claimed, and aptitude tests designed to show manual dexterity in simple tasks. There are some also designed to test reasoning ability like (intelligence tests) and those designed to indicate the possession or lack of certain character traits (personality test) need to be carried out by qualified personnel.

APPOINTMENT

Now that you have passed your interview and are considered for appointment after the final selection processes you will now be informed by telephone (or intercom if already an employee), but even if this is done, the appointment should still be confirmed in writing. The *"letter of appointment"* will state the date on which the successful candidate will start work, and the time at which he should report and to whom. The letter may contain, or be accompanied by, particulars of the *"terms and conditions of employment"*, such as hours of work, starting salary, holiday entitlement, commissions and/or bonuses, benefits, etc. A copy of the relevant job description may be given at the same time.

Unsuccessful candidates are not left out as they must be informed of their failure as early as possible by tactfully worded letters which ease disappointment and avoid upsetting the recipients. It must be remembered that although the candidate was not found to be the most suitable for similar or another post, it may be that the person concerned could be suitable for a similar post or another. It is, therefore, useful to retain the notes, etc, about those interviewed so that if possibly suitable vacancies arise in the future, the relevant previous candidates can be contacted at once. It may also be for the reason that (as mentioned earlier-on on page 6 last paragraph) the one(s) that was once found suitable or even appointed for the job have turned down the offer. This could help to fill the vacancy quickly without, perhaps, the necessity to waste money advertising again, and/or, to conduct another time-consuming session of interviews.

Once a vacancy has been filled and appointments have been made, it will not be over yet; the interviews and selection are **not** the end of the process as far as the successful candidate is concerned. There is no way of being certain at that stage whether the most suitable or correct selection was made

The next steps are *induction* – and that is the introduction of a "newcomer" or "recruit" to the organization – and *training*.

CHAPTER 14

INDUCTION PROCESS

The arrival of a recruit or a group of newcomers – sets in motion a process called **induction**. This is the process of introducing each recruit to the enterprise, and to the particular department(s) to which he or she will belong. Induction is really the beginning of the recruit's training, and should be clearly be defined. It should be enable a newcomer to become familiar quickly with the environment in which he or she will work, and the types of people to be worked with.

Proper induction process must never be overlooked; therefore, it is very important. The fact is that the quicker the recruit settles in and *"**feels at home**"* the quicker will that person be able to be worked with and start performing properly.

Regarding senior posts, induction must never be conducted by anyone who is junior or subordinate to the recruit, otherwise, it will serve only to embarrass the newcomer. However, if this happens with you, just ignore it, as it might have been done out of ignorance. Therefore, you should just compose yourself and move-on with your intended work. Not overlooking the fact that it is also the duty of personnel department staff to conduct induction processes even for some senior posts, however, it is not proper if the recruit's duties will involve supervising personnel department staff. Induction process should always be **well planned**.

INDUCTION PLANING

Officials who will conduct the induction process should obviously be aware of the day and time that the newcomer is to report well in time so that they may have ample time to officially inform of such event those that the recruit is going to work with.

The personnel department or an executive's secretary should have a diary note and should remind those concerned; as it is hardly helpful if the department manager looks up from his desk early in the morning only to find – unexpectedly – a nervous, and probably embarrassed 'new recruit' hovering at his door not knowing what to say or to do next. The manger should have known to expect a newcomer, and should have given instructions for him to be met by his secretary or one of his subordinate (who will always be senior on position to the recruit) at the main entrance and conducted – in a friendly, welcoming way to his office. It is also a good idea to warn and advise those with whom the new comer is to work with to welcome the recruit and provide a friendly atmosphere. With some companies' policies it is a punishable offence to embarrass a newcomer.

The impression, especially the first one, gained by a newcomer about the work atmosphere and about workmates (of whatever status) of the team or department and impression that the newcomer makes about those people – are important and can greatly influence him. New recruits, particularly the young and those starting their new first jobs, are likely to be anxious and apprehensive. They are also likely to be embarrassed by their lack of knowledge about the people with whom they are going to come into contact, and nervous about being in unfamiliar surroundings (unless they have been promoted or transferred from a close section or department). The induction process should therefore seek to put the newcomer at his or her "ease" as soon as possible. Simply being expected can bring relief; and a friendly welcome will also reduce tension. Depending on the size and the organizational structure, the new comer may first be introduced to the manager (in smaller enterprises) or to his departmental and/or section manager; even though they may have met previously – at an interview perhaps – a more relaxed introduction and a brief chat can do much to give a newcomer some confidence.

Work to be performed and information about the organization will, of cause, have been given at the interview and in any literature sent with the appointment letter. Some large organizations produce pamphlets or booklets containing much information of value to new employees, e.g. about remuneration and promotion policies, welfare and recreational facilities, etc. However important facts should be repeated, either by personnel department staff or the section/department manager concerned, and the newcomer should be encouraged to ask questions.

JOB INDUCTION

As mentioned above; the person who will be most intimately concerned with the job induction of a junior will be his supervisor or team leader in whose team the newcomer will work; with more senior posts it may be the section manager or even the department manager himself. However, induction responsibility level goes higher depending on who is to be inducted, like for example; if a Sales Director is to be recruited, it will be the responsibility of the Managing Director or one of the senior Directors to conduct such induction process.

Let us assume that a supervisor is delegated responsibility of the job induction of a new employee, he must ensure that the new employee knows his name and how to contact him; if necessary these facts should be written down especially his name which one can easily forget and feel embarrassed asking for it again. The supervisor must then ensure that the newcomer is aware of all facts concerning business hours, tea break hours, lunch time and so on.

Like we do to visitors at home; newcomer should then be shown around the department with emphasis on the section on which he will work, and on the location of the entrances/exits, toilets/cloakrooms, fire appliances, the canteen and drink dispensers, etc. the newcomer will also need to know, as appropriate from where to obtain stationary, literature, information, the location of machines, how spares are obtained, work tools which he may have to use and so on. If a personal locker is provided, its location should also be pointed out.

The location newcomer's desk if he is to work from office – or his work base and the surrounding furniture and area are, of course particularly important to insure that all necessary "accessories" which will be needed (e.g. pens, pencils, clips, note pads, and so on, as appropriate) are available – it is surprising how often such items "disappear" during a time a post becomes vacant! Not forgetting that a company can employ a disabled person; his or her condition must well be catered for and specialized entrance/exit points should be shown if one is to use a wheelchair or clutches. It important that a company make available any such specially made tools and accessories meant for their disabled members of staff. A newcomer could become very embarrassed by having to ask such "mundane" items if they are not available – would defeat the whole object of the induction process.

It is important that during the 'tour of inspection' the newcomer may be introduced to the people with whom he might have to come into contact again. Care must be taken a few newcomers can grasp names or put names to faces at one time – and designations or status of the persons concerned will also have to be learnt , eventually. It can save embarrassment and upsets if the newcomer is given guidance on the grades of people who may be addressed by their first names and those who should be addressed by their family names, with Mr, Mrs, Ms or Miss (or equivalents in the country concerned (as it differs country by country) as may be appropriate. There is less formality in some enterprises, or sections of them, than in others, and a newcomer who is aware of the situation will be more confident.

It is most likely, that, most of the people met during the "tour" might, of course, have been members of the department with whom the newcomer is to work with; but, in any case, special attention must be paid to his introductions to all such personnel, as it is important that they accept him into the group or team as early as possible. Either first names (or nicknames) and family names should be stated, and their jobs described briefly and, if convenient, a few minutes friendly chat may be encouraged.

CHAPTER 15

INTERNAL TRAINING PROCESS

No matter how educated or qualified one is; there is still need for a newcomer to receive some internal training so that one can fit-in well and have knowledge of that particular company's policies and regulations. However, the extent of training required by a particular recruit will depend on the seniority of the post, the duties involved and/or the method of work to be employed, prior practical experience possessed, and so on. For example:-

- A new assistant sales manager or field force supervisor or team leader/foreman require some managerial or supervisory training in addition to training on the method employed on the work to performed and will also have to be taught all about the company's organization, its policies, etc.

- An "internal" recruit, e.g. one recruited from within the same department or promoted/transferred from another department or branch may require less training (and induction) than a complete newcomer, depending on his past experience and what his new duties entail.

- An already experienced recruit will still need "re-training" on some aspects: on what ways his new work will now require differ from that which he used to work.

- Obviously the training of a junior or a complete new beginner will be very deferent from the foregoing, and will have to start from the "basics"

Of course, the training of one recruit will probably be easier, and on a more personal basis, than if a group of newcomers – possibly intended eventually to do deferent method of work – has been recruited at one time. In this section I shall concentrate on the latter situation, although what is taught – to an individual or to a group - is likely of necessity to be similar in many cases. (for simplicity, I refer to those given training as trainees)

Thus, having helped trainees to "feel at home" in their new surroundings, they may be escorted to the room where training will take place. A department manager should prepare an itinerary that will seek to indoctrinate the new recruits into the ways of the enterprise in general and with the policies of that particular department.

Ages will most likely to be deferent on recruits and may have had varying degrees and experience, so, it will be necessary for the department manager to "begin from the beginning" so that he caters for those with lowest level of knowledge. The trainer should ask questions to his class, and the answers received will indicate to him who of the new recruits is intelligent, confident or experienced. He should also note which recruits remain silent, and then frame questions which should be directed at them, in turn, so that they be obliged to reply – even they are embarrassed, nervous or unable to give a coherent answer. He should try to help them by remaining calm, polite and friendly, and by going over particular subjects again until the points discussed have been grasped.

He should avoid boring the more knowledgeable ones by asking them to write questions to which they would like answers to be given. This device could keep them interested and fully alert as each would try to write down the greatest number of intelligent questions.

Trainees should be warned against promising more than the enterprise can provide. The trainer must urge his class to   make notes of important facts so that they can refer to them on a later date, in addition to the manuals and literature with which they are likely to be provided. Trainees will need to learn how to counter competition; they need to be able to present clear and concise arguments in a friendly, logical manner. One way of assisting trainees to gain such expertise and confidence involves role playing.

ROLE PLAYING

The whole object of role playing is to teach and bolster confidence as each person should be given the opportunity to perform and the performance thereof can be discussed and commented on – criticized in a 'constructive' manner.

It is essential that the exercise is well controlled, and care be taken **not** to embarrass or belittle any trainee. This is important with beginners, who may be shy of performing in front of others, or who lacking confidence yet – are hesitant in their replies or in reacting quickly.

At the conclusion of the day's training the trainer can ask for the papers used to be handed for inspection. It is most probable that the trainer will particularly be interested in the papers of those trainees who had written down reasonable questions to which they require answers. If those questions are intelligently framed, he would see that the trainees concerned were keenly interested and that they had inquiring minds; for which, in the subsequent training sessions he could perhaps separate them from others and give them more advanced training courses in a deferent room.

It all depends on the work trainees will eventually be required to perform and some products and posts require far more training than do others, remember –

training might last from between a few days or three weeks, until the minimum degree of proficiency had been attained by all. Again depending on the work, for which they were recruited, the more experienced recruits might be allocated districts or sections to work on their own, or to gain more experience – some may be set to accompany other existing and experienced staff. It is possible as a result of training that some, for various reasons, would fail to take up their appointments or the trainer himself may have the reasons why some may not finally take up their posts.

CHAPTER 16

BASIC PRINCIPLES OF MANAGEMENT

Here I would like you to visualize in the eye of your mind what and how you should expect to be handled by manager(s) and what is expected of you by management.

MANAGEMENT – WORKER RELATIONSHIP

Modern management is an ART that involves the provision of leadership for a group of people, together with the training, advice and guidance, supervision and control necessary for each individual in the group to perform his or her work in the best way.

And if the stated goal or objective is to be achieved, the work of each person in the group must be so organized and co-ordinated that they work together as a **team.** Just as basic materials an artist work may be his paints, and the porter's basic material is his clay, so does the manager have his much complex material – **human beings,** men and women. (It is worth remembering always that the first syllable of management is man). **Management is thus the art of managing the activities of other people.** This really is no exaggeration, and the measure of any manager's success – or failure –

depends to a great extent upon his skill in dealing **effectively** with other people.

Management seeks to ensure that a group of people work together in the most effective manner to achieve **a stated goal,** in the most economical way. Management is thus a job of work: but a job which is that much more difficult because it involves dealing with not inanimate objects, services or theories but with *unpredictable men and women,* each of whom has a deferent and complex character.

Having used the words "goal" and "team" I can examine further the objectives of management, using an example with which you are likely familiar – a football (soccer) team, such a team comprises eleven people: they do not simply walk to the football pitch, stand wherever they feel like and start kicking the ball in whichever direction they also feel like and at random – if they did so, they would stand little chance of beating the opposing side! **No!** Under the direction of the team captain, who is one of the eleven players, and the team manager (who may not be one of the eleven players and who may remain off the pitch) each team member takes up a predetermined position; where possible the position which, from previous position, he (or She) has been found to be most suitable. From prior training each player has been encouraged to improve his playing skills, and each will know his role is in the team as an attacker or a defender, for example – and know the rules of the game.

With the foregoing example – wherever possible, the team will try to play the game to a plan or a method laid down in advance by the team manager, and the efforts of the players on the field will be controlled and co-ordinated by the team captain, who will give additional instructions and take on-the-spot decisions as necessary. Because the eleven players form a **team** and are not just eleven individuals playing separately with the same ball:-

> ➢ they will pass the ball to team-mates;
>
> ➢ will try to create opportunities for them; and
>
> ➢ they will play **together** to achieve their objective – which in this case is to score goals against their opponents.

By giving guidance and encouragement, the captain and the team manager will motivate all the team members to do their very best to win.

Let us now relate the foregoing example to a business, bearing in mind that many professional football teams are run on business lines. The team manager would be the owner of the business, or a section, or a department who might not actually perform the work concerned, but who must possess considerable knowledge of the actual work to be performed. The equivalent of a team captain will be the supervisor or a foreman or an assistant manager or team leader who although subordinate (junior) to the manager will work closely with him. The players would be the members of staff of the organization, or the section, or the department of it. The objective of the organization, or section, or department may be the production of an item or the sale of an item, or provision or sale of a service, or field work in the case of and Non-Governmental Organization (NGO) or any public institution.

The manager and supervisor must ensure that members of staff are so organized that they work together as a team to achieve the stated objective. Each individual must know what he (or she) is to do, where, when, how and where possible he will be given work to do which he most suited to perform, and he will be trained to perform that work. The work of members of staff will be planned in advance and organized so that one is not idle whilst another is overloaded; their efforts will be co-ordinated so that there will be no hold-ups or delays and so that, if necessary, work flows smoothly from one person to the next. And, of-course the manager and the supervisor must be available and willing to advice, guide and encourage their subordinates.

We can take the example further by thinking of each team in the professional Football Association or League as a department of business, each having its own manager and supervisor (the team manager and captain respectively). The governing body – eg Committee or Council) – of the Association/League, which exercises control over all the teams involved, defines the policy and lays down the rules of the game. Is equivalent to the top management strata of a business, e.g, the top board of directors of a company. Indeed many large institutions/businesses are organized in a very similar fashion.

In many types of activity, the completion between the teams of workers employed by different institutions/businesses is "remote". For example the team of production workers under the control of the production manager will attempt to 'beat' the team of production manager of a competitive enterprise/institution by producing a better product, or producing it more economically.

Selling, however, is far closer to our football team example, as very often members of the one sales team are in "direct" – and sometimes even personal

– competition with other members of another enterprise's sales team, trying to sell the same or similar product to the **same prospects** (people who have intention to buy). A sales manager's sales team must "beat" or score goals against the opposing (competitive) team members by securing those prospects of as **customers** – making sales to them – and, however, possible by even "taking away" customers from competitive salesmen. What is more, they have to defend their positions by ensuring that they retain **their** customers, and prevent competitive salesmen "poaching" them away (which would be analogous to conceding a goal).

As earlier on mentioned in the opening of this chapter; management involves the provision of leadership for a group of people together with the training, advice and guidance, supervision and control necessary for each individual in the group to perform his or her work in the best way. And if the stated goal or objective is to be achieved, the work of each person in the group must be so organized, planned, co-ordinated, motivated and controlled.

GENERAL FUNCTIONS OF MANAGEMENT PLANNING

This entails deciding how the predetermined objectives of the business, or department of it, should be achieved in the most efficient and cost-effective way in accordance with the organization's policies.

ORGANIZATION

This involves putting the theory (the plans) into "practice" so arranging the work to be performed that the objectives will be achieved as laid down in the plans.

CO-ORDINATING

This is closely related to organizing, and ensures that although different staff performs work differently, all their efforts mesh smoothly together and are directed towards achieving the common objectives.

MOTIVATING

This involves providing leadership for subordinates, and it also requires the ability to inspire them to give their best in achieving the objectives, by creating a good morale or working spirit amongst all those employed.

CONTROLLING

This comprises supervising the people employed, checking their work (and any machines and/or equipment used), to ensure that the end result is the desired objective. It also includes the recording and/or analyzing of performances to provide a guide for future similar activities.

BUSINESS OBJECTIVES

You will have noted that the functions of management are all concerned with achieving objectives. Let us first consider what those objectives might be, and who decides what they are to be.

Basically, objectives are the **goals** which the owners/management of an institution/business aim to achieve; infect their attainment is the principal reason for the existence of that business/institution. Before any business is started or established, a person or a group of people have to decide what that business is going to do. Is it going to produce something – if so what? Is it going to buy and selling – if so what? Is it going to provide service – if so what?

In some cases the answer to such a question is straightforward. For example, a person may decide to open a book shop, or an experienced painter/decorator may decide to set up his own instead of working for others. However, in other cases considerable thought and research may be necessary before deciding to produce or to provide and sell something which is not already available. As you have already learnt in the private sector the specific objectives of a business are combined with the objective of profit; the result of achieving the specific objectives of the business must be that its owners **gain** profit.

BUSINESS POLICIES

Hand in hand with the decision on the objectives of an enterprise is the necessity to decide – in broad terms – **how** and **where** the objectives are to be achieved, that is, to lay down the basic **policies** of an enterprise. If the objective of a particular enterprise is to sell, then it must be decided how sales will be made: (for example, cash and/or credit) and where sales will be made: from shops or by mail order or travelers or door to door salesmen or in the case of service providers: mode and area of service and whether profit or non-profit service provision and how it will reach the intended beneficiary etc. , and of course where the premises of the organization will be located.

Once the initial objectives and basic policies of an enterprise/organization have been decided upon, the interpretation and implementation of the policies and the achievement of the objectives are the responsibilities of the management team. Although where will be objectives for the organization as a whole, there will be also departmental or section objectives set, with policies laid down for the attainment of them. Unless each department attains its set object, the objectives of an organization as a whole might not be achieved.

The basic objective of each department (or section) will be to perform to the maximum whether it provides services or it sells goods. The policies of the department or an organization as a whole will cover such matters as the method(s) by which duties will be performed, from where or in what areas or territories will be operated from. The **interpretation** of the policy laid down for the department, and its **implementation** to achieve that department's objectives, will be the **responsibility of the manager.**

PLANNING

Plans are routes to objectives, once objectives have been set, planning is necessary to work out how to achieve those objectives within the framework of policy formulated.

❖ The board of directors, top management, is involved mainly with long term planning or "strategic planning", which is concerned primarily with deciding what the objective(s) of an organization should be in two, five, eight or even ten years to come, and its future policies. Such planning is concerned is concerned with an organization as a whole, rather than with individuals or sections.

❖ Senior management is involved with "tactical planning", that is, planning how overall strategies are to be achieved; devising and operating short-term plans, for up to a year ahead.

❖ Other strata of management are involved mainly in **very short-term and activity planning or operational planning** involved with day to day running of departments or sections and with individual assignments, for example; planning how to make an approach with the recipients of your products or service, or design advertisements, or decide what each member of the workers should be doing at any given time

- ❖ A good deal of the planning which line managers are called upon to perform involves making routine and dealing with "everyday" matters, for example; planning the work of the work-force either in or outside offices, which will be similar week after week. However plans must be **flexible** so that they can quickly and easily be modified in the light of events. For example; a department manager might have decided how his office staff will cope whilst another member is off duty, and has planned re-arrangement of the work. Such routine planning will be an automatic process requiring little conscious thought on the part of a manager, as plans and decisions will be based largely on past experience with similar, or even identical problems.

- ❖ Other planning, however, may require far more conscious thought, and even investigation and research before decisions are reached; such as seminars or exhibitions or promotional campaigns.

ORGANIZING

Once the plans – theories – have been formulated, a manager is involved in organizing the physical resources at his disposal – the people, materials, machines and even premises – to ensure that the objectives are achieved as planned. Organizing involves much more than simply instructing a given number of people to start work.

- ❖ Each person must know exactly what he or she is to do (and if necessary must be taught or trained to do that work), must know how the work is to be done, where and when it is to be done, and so on.

- ❖ Any materials needed must be readily available, as must be all the services necessary: electricity, water, telephones, fax and internet machines and other facilities, etc.

- ❖ The best machinery and equipment, within the financial recourses of the department or organization should be available for use, regularly maintained and in good working order, and if necessary training must be given to those who will operate any such machines.

- ❖ The premises, whether shop, showroom, store, factory or office must be so laid out as to provide the maximum efficiency and convenience. The available amount of space must be utilized in the most effective layout, so as to avoid wasted effort, duplication and unnecessary movement.

- ❖ There must be adequate and competent staff to perform the work.

Organizing then is ensuring that the right staff, the right materials, and the right equipment are in the right places at the right times and in the right quantities so that work will proceed in accordance with the formulated plans, without unnecessary delays, hold-ups or stoppages.

CO-ORDINATING

The two functions of organizing and co-ordinating are very closely linked and frequently co-ordinating is an essential continuation of organizing. Co-ordinating involves ensuring that all efforts move smoothly together in the same direction, that is, towards the common objective. Co-ordination is as essential in top management as it is at junior management and supervisory levels. For example, the Managing Director (commonly referred to as "MD") or general manager must ensure that the efforts and activities of all the deferent departments of a business or institution are in harmony, and in co-operation. For example; there would be **no** value if the department endeavours to sell a product that is not yet in stock and available, and or roll out a program whose time is not yet come.

Good relations and communications between department managers must be developed and fostered so that executives work together in concert. Similarly, more junior managers, team leaders, supervisors and foremen must co-ordinate the work of their subordinates, so that although deferent people might be performing deferent tasks, work and information will, when appropriate, flow smoothly and continuously from one person to the next.

MOTIVATING

Motivation is directly concerned with the people who work for a particular organization, and involves encouraging them to work well and willingly in the most economic manner in the best interest of the organization. The objectives of an enterprise can be achieved **only** through the efforts of people; and people need to be motivated – induced, persuaded, prevailed upon (but not forced) – in a humane and understanding to give off their best.

However, you must appreciate that what motivates one or group of people might not motivate another. Therefore, in order to secure the best a manager should, as far as is feasible possible, get to know something about his subordinates. Mere financial reward is more of an incentive than a motivation to many people, all though the end result – greater effort or better performance – may appear the same.

Many people today are interested in gaining more from their employment than just money; they tend to look for what can be termed "job satisfaction", doing jobs which they enjoy, in which they fill that their skills/abilities are being utilized to the full, and of which the end products are worthwhile and are appreciated. Many are interested in the likelihood of receiving training, of working in a group, in the prospect for promotion, in achieving positions of responsibility and authority or status. Others may want jobs in which they can use initiative or can get away from "being desk bound" or being "tied" to a routine or to regular hours. (It must not be overlooked, however, that some employees are content with routine or repetitive work, and being allowed to remain on that type of work is in itself a motivation for them).

You can see that the range of motivation can be great, and of course more than one (different) motivation may stimulate a particular person or group of people. However, a manager must endeavour to get the best from **each** member of his team, and that may require motivating deferent members in deferent ways, whilst motivating **a team as a whole.** The latter requires the building of a **better** "working atmosphere" based on spirit of trust and co-operation between management and staff.

Good *"working terms"* help in generating a good working relationship. Junior managers or supervisors will, of course, have little control over terms and conditions (or say in the matter over salaries/wages, bonuses, commissions, overtime, holidays, etc.) Team members must, however, be able to trust their superiors to put their case, whenever possible, to their immediate superiors.

There must be **two-way communication:** that is, **information** (and not only instructions) must pass from employees to management. Staff must be kept informed of happenings which will or might affect their livelihoods. **Job security** is important in forming a good working atmosphere, and in encouraging personnel to work well.

Subordinates want to know that they are looked upon not as mere "work units" or "production units" but as human beings, and that their manager(s) are genuinely interested in them as such. They require –

and expect – an even-handed, fair, unbiased approach from their managers, in addition to that essential quality called **leadership**. It is important to appreciate that successful motivation by a good manager produces a good measure of self discipline in his or her team; they will have sufficient self respect, and loyalty to him to work well and willingly.

In conclusion we can say that effective motivation instills good mental working attitude towards work – which mere financial incentive cannot buy.

CONTROLLING

Controlling is the function of management which checks whether what was planned to happen actually does happen; and, if necessary, ensures that corrective action is taken. Within this framework it can be seen that the work of all personnel must be supervised and checked (and further instruction, guidance or training when required); and that all operations must be checked or inspected, and performance measure against the targets set in the plans.

Controlling ensures that personnel perform the work allocated to them in the ways laid down – and no wastage or duplication of time, effort or materials. This involves much more than simply instructing a single number of people to perform work; they must be supervised and managed so that their efforts achieve the desired results. And that requires, as already explained, that they be motivated, checked, guided, taught and encouraged.

An important part of the function of controlling entails the maintaining of records of performance. Such "records" are vital as a guide to future planning and in the setting of new or revised sales targets as well as in controlling the work-force.

I hope you are enriched and equipped well enough to face your next interview and job successfully.

Good Luck

I KINDLY WISH YOU SUCCESS.

AUTHOR –Sir Francis Mutimuri

REFERENCE P Allen-*Selling Management and Practice 1ˢᵗ Addition* p. 7

Lancaster, Geoffrey A and David Jobber - *Sales Techniques and Management 2ⁿᵈ addition 1990* p. 18

Stephen Dank - *Business Studies 3ʳᵈ addition* p. 3

Susan Hamond - *Business Studies* p. 1

CPM Volume One p 4

THE END

www.ingramcontent.com/pod-product-compliance
Lightning Source LLC
Chambersburg PA
CBHW050242220526
45465CB00002B/513